The little red book
of dancing...

Salsa!

...or "Everything Your Mother
Never Told You About
Salsa Dancing!"

Daniel Allen

Dedicated to Tanya

With many thanks to Anita, Ariana, Coco, Cristina, Dae, Doris, Fraudy, Gabriela, Graeme, James, Jenny, Joe, Juan, Karol, Laurie, Lilly, Louisa, Marc, Marieke, Max, Mellissa, Moro, Nikoletta, Rafael, Rebecca, Rie, Suyen, Trung, Valery, Yarima and anyone else who has helped, influenced, taught or danced with me over all these years…

Facebook: https://www.facebook.com/DanAllenBooks

Why do I dance?

...and why did I

write this book?

I was a professional musician (...well, actually a drummer, if that counts?) but as I grew away from performing, and eventually from even playing anymore, I began to hang around the salsa dancing scene as it was great music (I have always loved salsa... I grew up around it and played in several Latin bands). Everyone was friendly and sociable, up doing something energetic, exercising and having fun! I realised (and I know this is going to sound corny and cheesy!) but I wanted to join them and 'play' my body as an instrument dancing to the music.

I began by tapping my feet to the rhythm as I would have playing drums, and then moving my arms to the music's 'accents' as I would have hit cymbals, cowbells, etc. and then eventually realised I had to transform this somewhat 'odd' dance style into a more socially defined and acceptable recognisable dance pattern, so I started taking salsa lessons to learn to dance as a couple with a partner. As I said, I had grown up around Latin music, therefore I had seen salsa dancing, but as a 10 year–old boy, I was too 'cool' to dance and thus did not really know any of the moves. I had to learn to channel my rhythmic expressions into more standard movements that other dancers could understand and follow.

I also grew up kind of rough, and didn't really like people touching or hugging me, so I have sort of used dancing as self–therapy to learn to get more close to complete strangers, and even friends... In fact, my friends teased me when I started dancing that I only liked to touch my partners with one finger – like they had 'girl–germs' or 'cooties'! I quickly became more comfortable with close–hold dancing and using my arms and body to lead.

I wrote this book as I feel there are a lot of things I had to 'discover' or teach myself that were not discussed in dance classes (after all, dance is an activity, and people go to dance class wanting to learn to 'do' something – not sit around and talk about it) or that I have learnt from friends that helped me to understand the 'how's and why's' of dancing... I am hoping to share these on with you in one simple collection of tips, ideas, suggestions, advice, explanations and above all –

encouragement! Dance is an amazing journey of self–exploration that can build a person's confidence, acceptance of themselves (and their bodies) and happiness... I have seen people transformed into new, more confident, energetic, happy people that socialise more, are more active, and have more fun!

I had two salsa teachers once...one who would just say, "do this" and another who would tell us the complete history and evolution of every move. I appreciated both very much, but have found the one thing lacking in dance classes (and it's understandable as people are there to learn to 'do' something) is the kind of theory, or reasons why you might do something – the 'background' material so that it all makes sense. I wanted to create a collection of tips, hints, insights, encouragement and advice I have, or received, into one book that will hopefully help others in their quest to not just dance, but to understand... live it... breathe it... and feel salsa! I hope you will too!

Even if you are just learning salsa to try and pick up hot chics, or cause your girl–friend or wife wants to so you have to, this book can help you realise it is a personal journey of self–awareness and confidence building that can transform your life – not just on the dance floor, but at work, in social circles, your creativity and interests and much more...

Good luck, and have fun!

CONTENTS

DANCING &
WALKING

Dancing is walking... if you can walk, you can dance!

Like learning to walk, once you know how, it is automatic and you can enjoy the scenery, have a conversation, etc. Learning to dance is the same – it becomes what they call 'muscle memory' and you don't need to think 'left, right, left...' etc.

Imagine facing your partner and simply stepping, or walking, forward and backward. It's easy – take one step forward, return to centre, then one step back, and return to centre again. Very easy! Now, just add a little flair, some turns and spins, enjoy yourself and you are dancing!

Salsa is a partner dance – whatever the lead does, the follow should 'mirror'. You can dance salsa alone (many people do at concerts) or sometimes two partners can dance 'solo' together, just doing fancy 'shines' or moves independent of each other, but it is meant to be a lead–follow dance between two people. (Sometimes a good lead can even dance with two followers at the same time!)

But back to the basics… if the lead steps forward, the follow should step back… and vice–versa. Partly for this reason, salsa is taught using an 8–count system. This is because salsa music generally has an 8 beat phrase (as opposed to Western music, which usually has 4 beats, or sometimes even just 3 beats). In salsa, there is a 'call–and–response' pattern in the baseline, claves, etc. that goes across 8 beats, so it is natural to dance to it in 8 beat segments. So, in most classes it is taught counting 1, 2, 3… 5, 6, 7.

In Latin America, you do not usually hear this counting, as most Latin Americans learn to dance 'naturally', or just growing up with it from friends and family who don't count at all when dancing. If they do, they might simply say 1, 2, 3… 1, 2, 3… as it doesn't really matter to them that much which beat they start on in relation to the 8–beat phrase of salsa. In fact, they can pretty much begin dancing on any beat they like, according to the specific type of rhythm in the style of the song… but more about that later in the Musicality chapter.

So therefore, if you take a salsa class, or just teach yourself watching videos on the internet, you will probably be counting in 8 beats. But, in salsa, we really only use 6 of those beats to step on – 1, 2, 3 and 5, 6, 7. What happens to beats 4 and 8? Nothing… it is a 'ghost' step – a 'rest' or 'pause' in the dance. As you progress and become more comfortable and confident with your salsa, you may begin using that pause or 'break' in the dancing to add accents with your body, such as foot taps, body drops, head snaps, shoulder shakes, etc., as the rhythm of the song calls for in that style of music.

For example, it is very common in Cuban style of dancing, to have a light 'tap' leading into the next step on 4 and 8. This 'tap' happens with the same foot that you will then step on, so the tap is like a little warm–up or 'pre–step' for the next step. It is easiest to think of 'tap, 1, 2, 3' and 'tap, 5, 6, 7' when you are first learning to do this.

So, for the lead dancer, it will look like this:

1 – step left	5 – step right
2 – step right	6 – step left
3 – step left	7 – step right
4 – TAP RIGHT	8 – TAP LEFT

WARNING: once you begin tapping, or accenting your dances

on the 4 and 8, it is very hard to go back to not tapping. It becomes second–nature, like breathing, and most of the time you are not even aware that you are doing it.

I once took an LA style class to brush up on my linear moves, and I was constantly getting in trouble for doing my 'Cuban' taps on 4 and 8 in the class. I couldn't help myself – it was just instinctive to add in these little accents like body, drops, head snaps, shoulder shimmies and taps on 4 and 8.

In LA style, it is a more fluid, even stepping – just like walking: left, right, left, right... you would never walk : left, left, left, right!

Just a quick 'foot'–note; speaking of walking, you need good shoes to walk in... similarly, when you first begin, dancing shoes make a world of difference! I can't recommend highly enough that you get a pair... then, when you are more experienced, you will learn to dance in any shoes (runners, sandals, etc.) on any surface (sand, grass, cruise boats)

...and an 'other foot'–note: Most LA style followers wear high–heel dancing shoes, whereas Cuban followers will generally tend to wear flat or street shoes. This is partly because of the fact that LA Style involves a lot of spinning, whereas Cubans 'step' through their turns and don't spin on the spot on one foot. I think this is why I may have a subconscious preference for

Cuban dancing as well... when a woman steps on you with the spike of a high–heel going into the side of your ankle, you might start thinking about switching to Cuban too!

WHY DANCE?

If this chapter seems obvious to you, then you can skip it... I've included it for a specific reason – you're going to want to take a break from learning to lead salsa at some point (even if only for a few days...) so you need some reasons to remind you why you are dancing.

The #1 reason to keep dancing is because you like it: the feeling of a good dance, the right song, partner, room on the dance floor, etc. that makes everything seem effortless – like you're flying... I used to perform in a band and the nights (or just a few songs sometimes...) when we were all in sync in the same groove, with an appreciative crowd, great sound support and in a cool club made it all come together in the same way – effortless, floating on air, in the groove, at one with the world!

I used to race mountain bikes and I remember the same feeling flying downhill in a good race – it's addictive: you'll want to keep getting that feeling! It's called a 'sweet spot' or 'in the groove' – most every sport or activity has its own where everything comes together into one amazing feeling... sailing, singing, swimming, skiing... and salsa dancing!

Some more reasons to keep dancing are that it has been scientifically proven to be good for you! It can make you:

Smarter

A recent study into preventing dementia (published in the "*New England Journal of Medicine*" [1]) tested a variety of "physical and cognitive activities that influenced mental acuity" [2], and found that "the only physical activity to offer protection against dementia was frequent dancing".[2]

In fact, so much so, that the results (as reported in an article from *Stanford University*[2]) are summarised below by order of reduced risk of dementia:

Playing golf – 0%
Bicycling and swimming – 0%
Reading – 35%
Doing crossword puzzles at least four days a week – 47%
Dancing frequently – 76%

Happier

Reduces stress, tension and depression as it introduces you to a social circle of other people with similar interests.

Healthier

Strengthens bones and muscles (usually without hurting them!) and improves posture, balance and flexibility. Also builds endurance and stamina, is the most calorie burning social dance after aerobics, and you can detox from all the sweating!

Confident

I have personally seen and known men who were shy, timid and self–conscious develop into confident, proud, fun guys directly as a result of their learning to dance.

Plus, you get to be a part of a great group of people all doing something they love, keeping fit, not drinking and eating all night, meeting people and making friends, dancing and listening to fantastic music – even at live concerts, as well as something you can do anywhere in the world. I love seeing what the salsa scene is like around the world when I travel. I remember the craziest was when I was in Prague and they still smoke in clubs there, so quite often you would see a lead dancer with a shot of 'slivovic' in one hand and a cigarette in the other... when they wanted to turn a follower, they would put the cigarette in their mouth and turn her with their free hand! I had female friends there who said they hated coming home with ash in their hair from being spun around into cigarettes!

But I digress... so when you start feeling a little disillusioned, tired of trying, or just need a little break – don't give up! It will get easier and more fun as you progress along. I remember when I had my first 'sweet spot' dance where the whole song was 'in the groove' and the rush I got from it has always kept me coming back for more! I know it can seem far and few between sometimes, but the only answer is to keep dancing (or start dancing more!) and it will happen more often...

Footnote 1

Leisure Activities and the Risk of Dementia in the Elderly

Joe Verghese, M.D., Richard B. Lipton, M.D., Mindy J. Katz, M.P.H., Charles B. Hall, Ph.D., Carol A. Derby, Ph.D., Gail Kuslansky, Ph.D., Anne F. Ambrose, M.D., Martin Sliwinski, Ph.D., and Herman Buschke, M.D.

N Engl J Med 2003; 348:2508–2516June 19, 2003DOI: 10.1056/NEJMoa022252
http://www.nejm.org/doi/full/10.1056/NEJMoa022252

Footnote 2

"Use It or Lose It: Dancing Makes You Smarter" by Richard Powers, July 30, 2010
Copyright © 2010, 2013 Richard Powers, from:
http://socialdance.stanford.edu/syllabi/smarter.htm

LA vs. CUBAN

I think dancing is dancing – whatever dance you do, that's the best dance for you!

Having said that, I am aware that there are two main styles of dancing salsa – LA and Cuban. When I say LA style, I mean linear, and thus also include NY and On2 Mambo, Puerto Rican and Miami styles, even though those are quite different sub–styles of liner dancing, they are still within the linear family, as opposed to the Cuban family, which includes Rueda.

I personally started with LA, and then learnt more Cuban and found that I could lead an LA woman better with Cuban, than I could lead a Cuban with LA, so I stayed with Cuban... plus, you have the added advantage of being able to dance Rueda!

(...more about Rueda in a minute.)

To be honest, I see the main difference in the attitude... I think LA style is meant more for show. I draw the analogy that LA style is also called linear since it is danced on a line, with either partner always on this 180° straight line, which in my opinion, lends itself quite easily to being danced on stage as a performance where you can always see both partners on each side of the stage. Cuban however, is danced in a circular motion where each dancer is constantly moving around each other. Also, the way Cubans hold each other dancing doesn't really lend itself to fancy hand movements by the followers. However, as a Cuban friend of mine put it once, Cuban women dance with their butt's – they show them off and move them a lot more than LA style dancers ever would... I find that Cubans also tend to not think (or care) what anyone is thinking about them – if they want to do something, they just do it!

Another major difference between LA and Cuban salsa dance is obviously the music style. Cuban tends to be more based in African musical roots and has more Rumba, Timba, Mambo and even Reggaeton breaks in the music that lend well to the Afro–Cuban dance moves. LA style salsa music (which includes the NY Mambo and Puerto Rican styles) is much more 'pop' and has a consistent beat that doesn't really break into Afro–Cuban music styles as much. I also find LA and NY salsa music does not have the typical 'call–and–response' bass and rhythm patterns that Cuban salsa does.

It is also very interesting to me that it seems like most LA and Cuban dancers will count the opposite beats in the music. For example, in the same song, LA dancers and Cuban dancers will both count the '1' beat differently – one style will say 1 is on the 1, and the other will say 1 is on the 5. It is especially noticeable when beginning a Rueda (where everyone has to dance to the same 1 beat to be in sync) when you might see LA dancers and Cuban dancers each dancing to a different 1 and 5 beat.

There is no right and wrong to this, (except in Rueda!) as each lead dancer should dance to his (or her) 'beat'. When you are social dancing as a couple, it should not make any difference (as I will go into in the chapter on Musicality, a lot of dancers start on any beat they like...) but again, in a situation like Rueda dancing, it is very noticeable and I have often wondered why LA and Cuban dancers hear the same music so differently – it must be the attention to the claves, conga, bass line or even just whenever the singer starts... I am sure everyone has their own 'style' of listening, and they're all fine!

Personally, I like the tonality and African based syncopated rhythms of Cuban salsa music, and sometimes it is more fun and interesting to dance to, as you can vary your dance style up to 3–4 times during one song. I think it is wonderful that anyone can dance any style of salsa to most any type of salsa music (including many other sub–genres like Columbian boogaloo!).

I have also found that I can lead an LA style follower in a Cuban style lead, and she will be fine with it. In fact, one of the best dances I've ever had was with a woman I didn't know who asked me to dance (so I know she had been checking me out...) and as soon as we started dancing I realised she danced LA style. I thought, "Ok, she must have been watching me, or she wouldn't have asked me to dance, so she knows I dance Cuban style... so I am just going to keep doing my thing and see what happens". Anyway, I would lead her Cuban style, and she would finish each move LA style. So, in a sense, we had the best of both worlds – I would lead her to a simple, basic Cuban turn (Cubans do not spin) and she would end it with a double or triple spin. I thought it was great. She got to do what she wanted to, and I got to lead the way I wanted to, and in the end, we both had a great time!

On the other hand, I find that if you lead a Cuban style follower in the LA style, they will not be very happy. For one, Cuban is a much more 'hands–on' (and I don't mean that in a bad way!) that uses a lot of push–pull, elastic, rubber–band, momentum. LA style is much more gentle and delicate and can often be led with one finger. Also, if an LA style lead tries to spin a Cuban woman she will just give him the look of death and never dance with him again. A lot of Latin American women do not like being spun around like they do in LA style. When my auntie from Puerto Rico and I used to dance, she would raise her finger and wag it back and forth at me and tell me, "Don't you spin me!"

Another nice advantage to leading Cuban style is that you can also dance Rueda, which is a circular Cuban folk dance in which a leader calls out a move and everyone performs the same move at the same time and then swaps partners. If you can imagine a circle of couples all dancing the same, and all the followers moving inside the circle and then changing partners as they move around the circle – it is very fun and beautiful to watch, but you must know Cuban salsa to dance it.

MUSICALITY

Musicality has many parts; it's not just finding the beat, but also dancing to the phrasing and different styles in the music as well.

Finding the beat

As mentioned before, everyone has a different way to 'hear' the beat. It can be from listening to the claves (which can invert), congas, bass line, or just the singer. I personally think that whatever you hear the beat as, is what you should dance it as. Reason being; except for Rueda, you are the leader and whatever you say/do goes... I know this sounds macho/sexist/whatever, but in partner dancing, there can only be one lead – and you're it! I think it's better if you generally find the same beat as everyone else, but theoretically, your follower should 'follow' you to any beat you want, as long as

17

you are consistent – you cannot keep jumping from leading on the 1 beat, to the 5 beat, to the 2 beat, etc. So, whatever beat you want to dance on, you'd better be good at finding and keeping it.

However, if you do get off beat dancing (...or if she is off beat!) don't stop dancing, don't apologise and DON'T tell her she is off beat... just break away from her, do a backward turn, a few shines or some rumba – whatever you want to... and when you are ready make a very strong accented entry back to couple dancing on the 1 beat (I usually hit my left foot hard on the floor on 1, but not while looking at her or anything, just as an accent hit to mark the beginning of partner dance again). If she is having trouble finding the beat, you can also try getting her into closed position to help 'guide' her back onto the beat.

Practice with a song

A pretty wild, fast and crazy syncopated song that has a very strong cowbell to help you practice finding the beat is "Flauta y Trombone" by "Los Dueños del Son", on the album "Dimelo! Con Salsa".

You should be able to hear, and hit, the 1 & 3 with your left foot on the first two beats of the cowbell, and 5 & 7 with your right foot on the second two beats. Don't try and do anything else – just get those strong hits. You should start to get the feeling of 'slowing down' the music and dancing more to the 'phrase' than to the beat (1, 2, 3... 5, 6, 7). This will also help you dance to a faster song with a more relaxed style that gives you plenty of time to do even complicated moves quite quickly.

But it leads us into our next bit about Musicality...

Dance to the musical phrase, not the beat count

You should dance to the overall rhythm, not to the beat count.

Try and think of the music as a 'phrase' or 'question–and–answer' / 'call–and–response', so that you set up a move and she completes it as a 'conversation' – not as 1, 2, 3... 5, 6, 7.

This will make you smoother and also give you a lot more time and room to dance as you are thinking in the big picture instead of the little beat. For example, I believe my job is to lead on 1, 2, 3 and then let her follow through on 5, 6, 7. I know this seems simplistic, and in some moves, unrealistic, but for the purposes of learning musicality, bear with me... Imagine asking her a question on 1, 2, 3, and then listening to her answer on 5, 6, 7... but in the big picture of a 'question & answer' – not by counting 1, 2, 3... 5, 6, 7. This way you will hear just the question and answer, and have lots of time and space within it to ponder, improvise, think, elaborate, etc. in your dancing.

Dance to the style of music being played in the song

Listen to the song's changing music style and dance moves that reflect it...

The song's music should dictate what you do when dancing, but in general, try something like this to get your started: (a very popular song that might help with this example is "Un Monton de Estrellas" by Polo Montañez on the album "Guajiro Natural" or "Oiga, Mire y Vea" by Grupo Niche).

At the beginning of the song (usually an intro to set the fell of the song) dance close and slow – get to know each other's rhythm, balance, style, etc. Smile at her and maybe even say 'hi'.

As the song progresses into the first verse, try a few simple moves – don't go straight into your best moves yet – save something for later to 'wow' her with...

Although personally I don't like thinking of salsa as sex, but if it helps, think of it like seduction: if you were kissing a woman for the first time, you wouldn't just go immediately straight in for the kill... salsa is the same – warm up with a little 'foreplay'.

When the first chorus comes, you can start some bolder moves

– again, not your fanciest , best moves yet, but just progress into a little more advanced ones – maybe intermediate level.

Then, there will usually be a break or bridge in the song – this can be fast or slow... so, go back to basics or close–hold dancing if it is slow... if it is fast, then you can try one of your fancy moves! If the music stops during the break, or radically changes the beat/style, you should definitely adapt to it – most followers hate when a lead just keeps continuing some choreo pattern or move right through a break in the music – if you don't know rumba or mambo or what to do, maybe just break apart and let her do a few of her own shines while you watch her.

When the music returns to the verses, again do your intermediate moves – there will be another bridge or finale later for you to let it all out and go crazy!

If you do all of this, you will not only show a little musicality in actually listening to the song you are dancing too, but you will also probably impress your follower with your 'respect' for them by letting them 'warm up' to you and your style before 'going in for the kill' and trying to impress her with all your fancy moves right from the start.

A dance doesn't have to be all about fast, fancy moves – going slow, having fun and making a connection can be much more rewarding to both lead and follower... sometimes the best dances are simple ones.

If it helps, here is a kind of sample visual map of a song:

Intro	Close–hold connection
Verse(s)	Simple moves
Chorus	Intermediate level moves
(Verse)	More simple moves (maybe a few new ones?)
Bridge/break	Either fast fancy moves, or break into rumba/mambo or shines
Verse	Again, simple moves (or variations on them?)
Chorus	Intermediate moves
Finale	Go crazy!

Give yourself a break – if the music breaks, you should too!

PLAY WITH YOURSELF

I rent a small local dance studio for a few hours every week (usually in the off–peak hours during the daytime or mornings) to dance by myself. I can't emphasize enough how much I feel this has contributed to my growth as a dancer. It sounds silly (what's the point of learning to lead salsa if you're just dancing by yourself?) but it is invaluable for your development as a dancer.

Here are some things you can try:

I pick one song I am infatuated with at the moment (it varies in tempo, style, etc. each week) and I repeat the same song for most of the hour. This is very important, because as you repeat the same move a few times you develop muscle memory so

23

that you don't need to think about it, and you can just enjoy dancing (like enjoying the scenery and conversation while walking). Other days, I will just play random songs I like and dance to all of them, but for these exercises, I find it best to find a song that matches what you want to do, and just keep repeating it.

Mambo

Find a Mambo song, or a salsa song with a strong Mambo beat, or even just a lot of Mambo breaks in it. I like "Ella Menea" by 'NG^2' on "Con Todas las de Ganar". Dance facing the mirror and do the standard Mambo pattern – left, left, right, right. Thrust your pelvis forward with each beat as far as it can go. You should be exhausted after one song, if not a third or half the way though it!

Next, after you are warmed up, start a new tap pattern:

left, left, right, left.

Then:

right, right, left, right.

Now start accenting different beats – first accent the 4 and the 8, so:

left, left, right, LEFT, right, right, left, RIGHT.

Then accent then 2 and 6, so:

left, LEFT, right, left, right, RIGHT, left, right.

(At this point, I might change songs and dance to "Que Bueno Baila Usted" by 'Oscar D'León' on "Aqui Esta La Salsa")

When you are comfortable with accents on 2 & 6, try dancing your salsa steps beginning on those beats. So, basically you will lightly tap on 1 on your left foot, and the step on 2 on your left foot, beginning the salsa sequence. Note: this is different to a Cuban tap on 4 and 8 – here you are 'tapping' on 1 and 5, and dancing on 2, 3, 4 and 6, 7, 8. It is simply an exercise to get you dancing on different beats. I personally feel much more 'space' in the music when I dance to beat 2 in this song – it feels like I have heaps of free time to do what I want compared to dancing on the 1 beat.

Now that you are dancing on beat 2 at this point, it is up to you whether you want to conform to the standard "On2" style and step back with your left foot on 1, and forward with your right on 5. It is up to you... my point is, you can dance on any beat you like (I have friends in Poland that dance on beat 3). You just have to know what you are doing, and again – be consistent! You can't keep changing the beat on a follower or you will drive her mad! I suggest you experiment like this with each song you dance to and see if you can find the 'optimum' beat that you like dancing for each song.

Contrary to what you learn in dance class, (they want to make sure that everyone is at least able to find the 1 beat... plus it's also easier for them to teach if everyone is in sync and start on the same beat) but it doesn't really matter what beat you dance to in salsa. In Colombia, I used to go crazy because the women just start on whatever beat they feel like and I used to have to try and figure it out and catch up! As, I mentioned before in the Musicality chapter, I honestly also believe that LA dancers and Cuban dancers hear the beat differently, but I don't want to go into this too much again, as you could probably write a whole book about it! You can dance to the bass line, the clave, the congas, etc. and it's all fine – there is no right and wrong! What I am trying to do here is to get you to be aware of what beat you are dancing on, and thus where the accents are, so that when the music tells you to, you can highlight them in your dancing!

Ok, I know I've said this before; it is the lead's right to begin leading on any beat they choose to, but it is also their responsibility to continue on that beat consistently for the duration of the song. So, dance with confidence that it is perfectly acceptable to begin on whatever beat you like, but you MUST continue on that beat throughout the song (with some exceptions, as some songs do have extreme rhythm changes, but even then, it will generally stay on the same beat). If you are constantly changing the beat that you lead on in a song, it will drive your follower crazy and she won't want to dance with you again... So, whatever you chose to do – just keep doing it!

More games

Pick a standard salsa song and begin adding an off–beat shine into your normal pattern. So, for example, in Cuban salsa, there is often a break (or accent) on 7 or 8. I often see Cuban dancers drop to the ground on 5, 6, 7 or 8 and back up on 1. Try something similar (dropping might be a bit hard to start) like simply standing on your right leg on 7 and holding it until you step on 1 with your left – kind of creating a pause or break in the pattern. Then try doing it from 5, and shake your shoulders (shimmy) on 6 and 7 before tapping on 8 with your left foot.

I am sure you can be creative and come up with more patterns like this. I like to experiment until I find ones that feel natural to me... I then try and incorporate them into my dancing when I am comfortable with using them. Practice makes perfect!

Now practice with a person!

Find a partner you can bring to the studio and practice with – ask a member of your dance class, or a friend, or even just advertise in the local adverts online. I often trade my 'practicing' on someone for my teaching them salsa, so you can find a friend who wants to learn and help teach each other!

HOW TO SURVIVE LEARNING TO LEAD

Why take the time, spend all this money, deal with all the stress of learning all the salsa stuff just so you can dance with someone?

Because dancing is fun!

Dancing has been scientifically proven to be good for you! It improves memory, thinking ability, reduces stress, makes you live longer, healthier and happier... and it's fun!

Why would you dance if it wasn't fun? Why would millions of

people throughout thousands of years dance if it wasn't pleasurable and enjoyable? I doubt it would have survived as a popular cultural and personal pastime if people didn't enjoy it, so my first two words of advice to you are: "Have fun".

I say this because I think it is often the most overlooked aspect of dancing – people take themselves too seriously, or are too stressed about looking good/knowing the right moves, etc., or are just forgetting what dancing is all about!

I know this sounds simple, but believe me, I have seen many men (and woman) never smile once on the dance floor. I know this is expected in certain dance styles like Tango, but in salsa, it IS expected! You must smile, and your partner must smile. Consider it your main job of leading to make her smile!

I hated leading when I first started salsa dancing. I thought, "this is unfair, I have to go to all the classes and learn all the moves and learn to protect the woman, smile at her, make her feel special, think of what moves to do when – what she likes and can or cannot do, and all she has to do is show up at the dance club and maybe say 'yes' if I ask her to dance" (which was a big gamble when I first started dancing!)

I learnt to like it as I realised that, just like women get lost in dance, we can too. I lead by feeling now, not thinking about which moves to do, or where to place her on the floor, I just 'feel' what she wants to do, and where she wants to go, and let her with my leading. I lead by feeling what she wants to do – I don't have to think what I want her to do.

I was initially attracted to Rueda for this reason. In Rueda, one caller calls out a move for everyone to do at the same time. I didn't have to think what to do! My point is, after you have gone through a period of 'thinking' about all this stuff I (and your teachers) are telling you, you will shut off your brain and start 'feeling' it – that is when leading becomes like following and you are both dancing 'together' and not leading/following.

ADDICTED TO SALSA

There was a funny thing going around Facebook a while ago that listed the several stages of addiction to salsa...

To paraphrase from memory:

First, you take a salsa class

Then you take a few classes per week

Then you start going out social dancing

So much so, that you need to cut back to work part–time

You only buy clothes and shoes that you can dance in...

...and then you think salsa is better than sex,

And suddenly you KNOW salsa is better than sex!

I think women get addicted to salsa much sooner than men do. A woman can begin social dancing with very few lessons (or none at all!). A man will need a lot more to learn to lead. Therefore, a woman has a head start on enjoying the freedom of salsa and becomes 'addicted' to it quite quickly. I had a female friend once who wanted to dance salsa everywhere we went, even if it was non–salsa club like R&B, Reggae, etc.

Anyway, men will eventually become as addicted to it once they learn enough leading to be able to relax and enjoy it. Stick with it, guys... it will all be worth it when you do.

KEY TIPS ON LEADING

Contrary to popular male beliefs, leading a simple basic dance with all of the elements listed below will be much more appreciated than trying to 'wow' her with a million complicated fast turns that jerk her around, get you off beat, and makes both of you stressed! Less showing off and more 'connection' should be a golden rule in salsa.

'Connect' with her

Smile and develop a 'conversation' of some kind dancing. At the very least, make her feel 'special' and don't look around searching for your next dance partner while dancing with her!

Protect her

Again, it should be obvious, but it's not – if you are looking at her, then protecting her should be a piece of cake. If you are not, then you won't even notice when she gets hit by someone or bumps into a post!

Be gentle with her

Never push, pull or force her! If you are, you are probably not leading properly – go back to the basics and focus on your connection again!

Be flexible

As mentioned above, if you do a move that doesn't work for some reason (you mess it up, or she makes a mistake, or you have to change it because someone else spun right into your space... don't panic and force anything – just smile and recover as best as possible. Never tell her she made a mistake or try and explain what she should do on the dance floor... and quite possibly, never even ever off the dance floor!

Meet her halfway...

After 5–10 seconds you should get an idea if she is a beginner or experienced dancer. If she is a beginner, meet her half way and do simple moves for her to feel good about herself and build her confidence, but also throw in a few more challenging ones that will impress her, not only with your lead, but with her ability to do the moves. Take it easy, don't go over her head!

Stay on beat

There is nothing more frustrating for a follower than to have to constantly stop dancing and wait for you to set the beat again... I find it's best to either keep dancing off the beat (if it's not that big a deal – just on the 5 instead of the 1, for example, might be passable...) or when the music permits you to (for example, as in a break or a bridge) then you can actually stop dancing or break apart and when you start again, come in on the right beat. Don't just randomly stop in the middle of dancing and stand there and then start again: use the breaks in the music to cover your mistake. A friend of mine once said that the best carpenters are ones that simply know how to hide their mistakes well – the same could be said of salsa leaders: if you get off beat or do a move that doesn't work out, don't stop and make it obvious, just continue and 'cover' it up.

LEARN TO LEAD

As I mentioned, this is not a 'step–by–step' book on how to learn to dance moves – rather a guide book of tips, advice and strategies for learning that are not usually mentioned in classes. So I won't go through each dance move with diagrams (that is what classes are for!) but here are a few things that I found greatly improved my leading skills

Learn to follow

I know you may still be learning to lead (and that is hard enough just by itself!) but if you can, have a try at following – it will teach you a lot about leading!

I help run a free social dance group that meets in the park on weekday lunchtimes and weekend afternoons, and one day we had many more men than women, so I offered to follow for anyone that would dance with me. At first, it was a bit hard to get used to, but I quickly just learnt to relax and 'listen' to what my partner was 'telling' me to do with their hands. I found some moves very easy to follow and others (which I had thought would be simpler) very hard. I kept with it for a couple of hours and by the end was 'dancing like a girl', as one of my friends put it. I was very happy though... I had experienced what it felt like physically, mentally and emotionally to follow for several different leads, as well as what moves are difficult for followers and which moves are heaps of fun! I found it an invaluable contribution to my skills and understanding as a leader and highly recommend it to everyone – remember, dancing is not about sex, and who you dance with has no bearing on your sexuality. I have danced with every type of follower there is: short/tall, skinny/large, male/female, beginner/experienced... and none of them had anything to do with my gender or sexual preference – dancing is about a conversation between two people: it doesn't matter what gender or sexual preference you or they are – you are just having a 'conversation'.

At the same time, if you are already dancing with a guy leading you, see if you can swap and have a try leading him. I actually used to dance with a bunch of my male teachers when there was a shortage of women in the class, and it's one of the best things I ever did to learn to lead. I hate to say it, but most women are so light and agile that you can pretty much make them do anything and not realise that you might be 'pushing and pulling' them around. However, most guys on the other hand are dead weight – big tree trunks that don't move very well... you can't turn a big man when his weight is on his back foot (not that it should ever be in dance, but when he steps back on one, his weight is shifted back). So, I really learnt the importance of feeling body weight and momentum from dancing with big guys, and to only turn them on 2 and 6 – never on 1 or 5!

Thus, I learnt never to turn a woman when she is on her back foot (with only a few exceptions like a couple's spin where we both spin on the spot if I step right next to her back foot) but in general, it taught me to 'feel' body weight and momentum, and to use it to my advantage, so that as I lead a woman, I am using her natural momentum to lead her, and not my muscles and strength.

Visualise your moves or routine... or just your dancing in general

Olympic athletes are able to completely imagine or visualise their entire gymnast routine, or bobsled run, or any other event... your dancing can be the same – if you can dance it in your mind, you can probably dance it on the dance floor. It is not necessary that you have a set routine to visualise – just try seeing yourself successfully completing the moves you want to (in detail, not just some romantic, blurry–visioned scene from a Hollywood movie). Theoretically, you should be able to lead an entire dance by yourself dong this without a partner. I find it a bit hard, as I use muscle memory and body momentum as crucial components of some moves, but I do know it is possible, and have seen some of my friends do amazing routines practicing alone. If it helps you get started, you can try dancing with a chair on top of a table that has a sweater over it so you have two 'hands' to hold.

When doing this kind of solo–exercises, make sure you are learning or doing the move correctly... I know from taking piano lessons that it is very easy to not see (or hear) a mistake you are making when practicing by yourself. A good teacher will always notice mistakes you aren't seeing... I actually tried the sweater on a chair exercise once and realised that I had ended up crossing the 'woman's' arms behind her back! Anyway, whatever works for you – visualising, practicing with a chair, dancing solo or with a friend who can keep an eye on any possible mistakes you're making, will all help your dancing immensely. Classes will teach you the moves, but like learning a language, you need to practice them daily. Even just 10–15 minutes a day, either mentally visualising them in your head, or as I do... dancing at the bus stop waiting for the bus!

Learn more moves

If you set yourself a goal of learning one move a week for a year, that's 52 moves! That's pretty good... I once figured out that if the average move is 16 beats long, and there are 400 beats in a short salsa song (Cuban salsa songs can go up to 6–8 minutes!) then you only need to know 25 moves to get through a song without repeating any!

If you are having trouble remembering all the moves you have learnt, try writing (or printing) them on large colour heavy–stock card paper. I then either tape them up on a wall in the studio I am practicing dancing, or just lay them on the floor. This will refresh your mind to all your possible moves. I also tried once making a flash–card slideshow on my laptop to randomly 'pop–up' a new move up for me to do, but found it was too much work to try and to sync it up in time with the music according to how long each move was, so in the end, it was becoming more like a choreo than a random flash–card slideshow, but you could try this for choreo if it works for you?

Also, I know people (and I have done this too) who either make a family–tree type list, or a graphic flow–chart mind map of moves and where they can lead to, as well as keeping a journal description of the moves and key elements or tricks for doing them. This really helps if you read or review it every day, imagining the move in your head – just like practicing words in a new language on a daily basis to increase your vocabulary.

Dance with your inner core

Turn on your core muscles when dancing – like most things you do, exercise, sports, etc., it is best done with your core muscles engaged: not only will this help you physically control a woman's centre of gravity and momentum, but it will also help her 'feel' your momentum – she can literally feel if you are 'engaged' or not and have your core muscles turned on.

This will help her 'feel' what you are leading, as your 'core' will be directing her as well as your hands. It will also help protect her by keeping her upright and steady, especially if she is a beginning dancer getting dizzy turning and spinning.

So remember, turn yourself on before you dance!

WHO & HOW TO ASK

Location, location, location...

Are they standing by the edge of the dance floor looking around or sitting in the darkest corner of the club farthest away from the dance floor? If they are at the bar, are they drinking a 'real' drink? (i.e. not water) chances are they might not want leave their drink unattended for a dance.

Women – make yourself available to be asked! Don't sit in the back corner talking to your girlfriends – stand at the edge of the dancing and actively make eye contact with someone you want to ask you.

The 'eyes' have it!

If you make eye contact with someone you know, a simple raised eyebrow or nod to the dance floor might be enough to signal a dance. If you don't know them, you should still get an idea if she holds your glance long enough to warrant your chances asking her to dance.

Look around the room for who you want to dance with and make eye contact with them BEFORE you approach them – if they return it, you will probably receive a 'yes' answer – if they look away, probably best for you to keep looking...

Just ask her...

I know it's hard being rejected, but just accept it – you are going to be rejected. There is nothing I (or you) can say or do to change this. I know amazing great leaders who have been turned down and I still can't believe it, but it does happen... I have been turned down, and even had a woman walk off the dance floor in the middle of a dance with me when I was a beginner. I was mortified and asked my friends if I literally stank, had stepped on her toes, touched her inappropriately by accident... and they said, no she's just a bit above the rest of us and every time I saw her that night she was standing by a pole not dancing... I don't think anyone of the regulars would ask her to dance.

Anyway, my point is, you're going to get rejected, not smiled at or thanked for a dance (hopefully not walked off of in the middle of a dance) so just expect it... I once got asked, "Can you dance?" when I asked a woman – I didn't know how to reply... I was not so sure of myself to say, 'Of course I can dance – I'm a great dancer!' So I just shook my head and walked away... I have had other guys say they get this question too, so I didn't feel too bad. I think women need to 'protect' themselves from bad dancers, and they also have many reasons for not wanting to dance with someone – body odour, height, how sweaty they are, if they are tired or thirsty and need a break, they don't like the song, or maybe they are waiting for someone 'special' to ask them to dance and don't want to be already taken... I have long ago since stopped trying to figure out what is wrong with me and just accepted that everyone will get turned down at some point or another... I found you can minimise the chances of this by presenting yourself well: clean, polite, smiling – but if it does happen, don't hold a grudge... just walk away and ask someone else... I've even heard of guys saying no to women asking them to dance, which I find incredible – if a woman has the courage to go out of her comfort zone and ask me, I will always try and say yes!

As usual, guys have to do all the work... asking a woman to dance, AND then leading her through the most amazing dance she's ever had! Just kidding... I know it's hard for guys to ask and be rejected, but here are some tips for minimising the rejection (as well as for women to increase their chances of being asked):

1) Not drinking, not smoking and not being rude. I was once in a dance hall and a man came in and stood next to me and said he was going to ask a 'hot chic' to dance some 'sexy Latin moves' with him and I could tell he was drunk (from the smell of alcohol and cigarettes on him) and I literally asked him please not to... I simply said "it's a complicated dance and someone might get hurt if you've been drinking"

2) Wear deodorant, bring an extra shirt (or few...) if you sweat a lot – guys might think a hot, sweaty woman is sexy, but trust me, women don't think the same! I was once sprayed in the face by the sweat from a woman's hair when I spun her... I was even temporarily blinded by it, but I honestly wasn't that upset. I just assume that we are all up being active, and sweat is going to happen.

3) Be polite, courteous and respectful... and look nice & clean – women have to judge you in an instant whether or not to dance with you when you ask them, so the better you present yourself as a nice clean, non–smelly, not–too–sweaty, nice guy – the better your chances!

Guys & gals – don't turn someone down for no reason!

If someone makes the effort to ask you, make the effort to dance with them – unless they smell, or are drunk or dangerous dancers who might hurt you, or grab you, or whatever... it is only polite to dance with someone who asks you. I am always amazed at the dancers I see turning people down and then standing there not dancing! Why do they bother coming out to a dance club?

A hint for women: don't ask a guy to dance – tell him you want to dance! Guys can get defensive if a woman seems to take the initiative asking, but they are used to women telling them what to do... so, don't ask – TELL him!

Anyway, if you are rejected, forget about it. Don't hold a grudge, or take it personally. Ask them again some other night (not on the same night) and if they still say no, then you can assume they don't want to dance with you. However, women take note; if you do this, people will notice it and might not ask you to dance if there is not a good obvious reason. I still think that a dance is only 3 minutes of your life – what else are you going to do in a dance hall besides stand by the pole at the edge of the dance floor for 3 minutes... wouldn't you rather be dancing?

I believe that every dancer can teach you something. I love dancing with beginners as they teach me to be a better leader. I also dance with amazing dancers, but to be honest, the best dances are just with the average, normal salsa dancers that just are there to have fun.

ETIQUETTE

Common sense may make these seem obvious, but it's amazing how often the simplest things are forgotten!

Keep your nails trimmed and use the palm or fingers to lead – not your fingernails – it gives the woman a better 'feel' of a hint what you want to do.

Be clean and smell nice. Keep a spare deodorant in your shoe bag. Bring 2 or 3 dry shirts (or wear a quick-dry non-cotton one). If you sweat a lot, hang a small towel in your back pocket to wipe yourself after every dance.

If possible, wear soft–soled shoes. I guarantee you are probably going to step on someone at some point (or be stepped on!) and the softer the shoe, the better!

Repeating moves...

> Once – to introduce the move to her
>
> Twice – to let her enjoy it and have fun with it
>
> Three times – she's bored and ready to move on...

Stand up straight. Provide a firm frame for her to follow.

Don't drink & dance. I know you might think you need a drink for courage and confidence, but like with most things that you do when you drink – only <u>you</u> *think* you are doing it better!

Protect her, respect her and treat her gently... enough said.

HOW TO DANCE SO THAT THEY WILL WANT TO DANCE WITH YOU AGAIN!

Smile at her

I know it sounds simple, but you'd be amazed how many guys forget (or are too nervous) to do this. I don't mean constantly force a smile on your face like a plastic mannequin – that gets creepy and freaks women out. Just flash a smile every now and then as you make eye contact. Again, you don't always need to look in her eyes, but you should always be watching her. It actually makes you a better leader if you actually watch her body movement and where she is, so keep an eye on her, and when your eyes catch, smile. Looking (and smiling) at her (and not all the other women on the dance floor!). This should come naturally – you should be having a good time, so 'smile'!

Make her feel special

Most women are as nervous or even more nervous than you are about looking like a clumsy idiot on the dance floor. You need to make her feel comfortable.

Protect her

A woman can actually sense, if not see, you scoping out the dance floor for a safe, open spot for her to 'perform' in. I don't mean just when you walk onto the dance floor, but as you are dancing and other couples are moving around you. I purposefully make a big show of a sweeping gesture with my hand in front of me, in an empty hole on the dance floor, to show her I have 'cleared' a spot for her to do an 'exhibela' or whatever solo spin/shine I want her to do. It shows her I have thought about her safety and have announced to the floor that she will be taking up this spot, as well as 'literally' setting the stage for her for everyone to look at her. You don't need to be this dramatic every time, but women will appreciate it.

Do moves she is comfortable with, and capable of doing

If a woman does not know or follow a move you try on her, forgot about it – do NOT try it again and then even worse, tell her how she is supposed to do it on the dance floor. I hate to say it, but chances are that you are not leading it properly, and it is not her fault anyway – sorry, but it's the hard truth. Instead, simply smile at her that everything is fine and forget about doing that move (or any similar ones) again. I dance Cuban, so if I try and ochenta on a woman and she does not seem comfortable with it (it is a hard move to follow for a beginner) then I do not do anything based on that move, such as an ochenta complicado, balsero, besito, etc. Remember, dancing is meant to be fun – if she doesn't know a move or seem conformable with it, don't push her – maybe next time you have a slower song together you can try again, but to keep trying in the same song, or as I said, even worse, to try and explain it to her during the song, is a huge turn–off for followers – imagine a woman stopping you dancing and telling you that you were leading wrong and showing you how to do it in front of everyone on the dance floor!

Also, don't do 'sexy' moves if she is not welcoming them. Women place their left hand in front of your right shoulder for a reason – to push you away! If you are getting to close or intimate with them and they feel uncomfortable, you should feel a gentle push against your right shoulder: this does not mean 'come closer' – it means 'back off'!

Be gentle and don't not 'jerk her around'

A good, confident leader will not pull or jerk a woman around. There is no need for physical force during salsa unless you are doing extreme choreo moves that you have rehearsed like flipping the woman over your head and sliding her between your legs as you hop on one foot. 99% of salsa dancing can be lead by the gentle nudge or tap on the shoulder or back – it is not about brute force. If you are dancing a fast song and think you need to pull her around to make her quicker, you are wrong. The best way to dance a fast song is to keep her closer to you, making her take smaller steps, and spinner or turning her tighter. If you do this, you can easily dance very fast songs with the gentlest of touch. I agree you will need momentum and a string, firm lead, but it is very different to jerking and pulling a woman around.

1, 2, 3... LEAD!

My theory on leading is you have until 3 to tell a woman what to do, and if you've missed it, go back to a basic or go with whatever she interprets your lead as. I love the concept that men lead and women follow – but men have to give women room to follow: the 5, 6 and 7 beats are hers – let her do her thing! It's like a call and response, question and answer... give her time and space to express herself.

Don't push & pull

This is especially important for dancing with a beginner. You might think that you need to lead them more forcefully and stronger than normal with an experienced dancer, but quite the opposite is true – you need to signal them strongly, but then be ready for them to do the opposite of what you expect (for any number of reasons) and relax your hold so that they don't hurt themselves turning the wrong way. Remember, it is a leader's job to lead on 1, 2 and 3 – and to let the follower follow on 5, 6 & 7. This way, you tell her what to do, and then she does it... if she doesn't do it, your job is over, she didn't get your message (or made a mistake in her following for whatever reason) but it is too late for you to change it – just relax and let her go do whatever she does and move on.

Don't teach on the dance floor

I am a firm believer in not repeating a move until she gets it, or worse, trying to explain to her what to do on the dance floor. Do not try to force women. If they aren't following properly, have a look at your own lead: ask your good friends if there is anything you can do to improve your lead – tell them that you have trouble leading a certain move and would like their feedback or help. Don't just assume that you need to be more forceful doing whatever it is you are doing – that's kind of like tourists who just shout louder in their own language when someone doesn't understand them in another language.

Look before you spin or turn her

I like to make a big show of my intention to spin or turn my partner so that everyone around me knows what I am going to do... so, when an empty space appears on the dance floor, I dramatically sweep my arm into it signalling that my partner will be entering the space as I turn or spin her into it.

Likewise, as you get better, you can use your peripheral vision to be able to start predicting what other dance couples are going to do around you – if you see a guy preparing a spin – watch out! Especially if it is an LA style one where the women fling their arms out with pointing fingers that can blind you!

Be ready to change your partner's direction and position at any time to protect her – scoop her out of harm's way if necessary! She will always forgive you (even for getting off beat!) if you save her from being collided into or stepped on by someone, and be very grateful that you 'rescued' her!

Dancing is a conversation

I would say the number one thing you are looking for in a good dance is a 'conversation' – a smile, an exchange of 'give and take' partner dance 'feel good' moves, some playful (and maybe even a bit flirtatious in an innocent way) 'banter'. A good lead is NOT about bossing her around, pushing and pulling her, literally 'telling' her what to do verbally... it is about 'listening' as well.

If you aren't quite sure what I mean by having a conservation dancing, I don't mean talking... I mean finding out what she likes – imagine asking her 'what do you like?" when dancing with her – if she smiles when you spin her, she likes that... if she resists your turns, then she doesn't... it's a conversation – ask her what she likes by trying something, and 'listen' to her body to see what she likes.

Lead like dating...

Like any sport, you wouldn't just rush into your most complicated moves without warming up... maybe the woman you have asked to dance has just arrived (or even just started dancing) and would appreciate a good warm up before being spun all over the dance floor!

Now, go get engaged!

Not literally... well, unless they're a great dancer!

RECIPE FOR A GREAT DANCE

Wash hands and body thoroughly

Trim sharp edges from fingernails

Apply generous amounts of deodorant to underarms

Groom well and wear nice clothes

Have 2–3 extra shirts ready for when you need them

Use your eyes to choose a good partner

Begin to slowly simmer

Don't forget to smile :)

As the music heats up, listen for cues to which spices you might like to add?

If it stops, remove from heat for a little break...

If it changes, make sure you stir accordingly

Finally, bring to a boil, but keep cover ready for safety

Relax, enjoy and always say 'thank you!'

THE LAST WORD

Finally, this is my last piece of advice, and I hate to say it cause it may seem to contradict most everything I have said in this book so far! I learnt the hard way that you have to dance for the reasons why you want to dance – not to please anyone else. If you want to have fun, have fun! If you want to show off, show off! If you want to pick up chics, pick up chics! I know this sounds contradictory or hypocritical of what I have been saying about pleasing your partner, making sure you think of their skills, desires, etc. and make them smile... but the point is, you are never going to please everyone – you can do the 'same' dance with two different women and one will love it and one might never dance with you again – you can't take it personally!

You need to just do what it is that drives you to dance and the rest will follow... (apologies for the bad pun!) I learnt that I want to dance to express myself to the music, kind of as a personal quest to be more comfortable and confident with my body. Again, as I grew up performing as a drummer in Latin bands, I was challenged by trying to make my body do what I wanted it to with the music as a dancer, not as a drummer, but I quickly tried to please everyone with my dancing and realised I am not here to make sure everyone has a good time, I am here to express myself! I obviously had to merge the two and not just swing women around like crazy if I felt like it, but my point is, that if you are true to yourself, and be honest about why you want to dance, then that will convey itself and people will respect it – if you just want to have fun, chances are, she probably will too... if you just want to show off, there are lots of women who would love to show off with you! And if you're just trying to pick up women, I am sure there are lots of women just dancing to meet a partner as well...

The point is, be honest and true to yourself and you will find where you fit in... the place that makes you happy dancing – but do always be considerate of other dancers, just remember that they are not all going to be looking for what you are – and while you might not make everyone happy, you need to find, develop and express your own style, but most importantly – have fun!

ABOUT THE AUTHOR

Daniel has played drums and percussion in Latin bands since he was 12 and has since directed his musical passion about salsa, son, rumba, timba, mambo, samba, forró and many more rythms into dancing. He now lives in Sydney, Australia, organising free social rueda and salsa dance groups in the parks, teaching as many people as he can to get up and dance!

21244988R00045

Made in the USA
San Bernardino, CA
14 May 2015